by Margaret Shanley

Consultant: Beth Gambro
Reading Specialist, Yorkville, Illinois

BEARPORT
PUBLISHING

Minneapolis, Minnesota

Teaching Tips

Before Reading

- Briefly discuss animal life cycles. Babies are born, they grow, and they have their own babies.
- Look through the glossary together. Read and discuss the words.
- Go on a picture walk, looking through the pictures to discuss vocabulary and make predictions about the text.

During Reading

- Encourage readers to point to each word as it is read. Stop occasionally to ask readers to point to a specific word in the text.
- If a reader encounters an unknown word, ask them to look at the rest of the page. Are there any clues to help them understand?

After Reading

- Check for understanding.
  - ▸ What are some things baby horses do during the first few weeks? What about after that?
  - ▸ Find a place in the book that tells you what a baby horse eats.
  - ▸ Look at page 22. What did you learn about baby horses from reading this book?
- Ask the readers to think deeper.
  - ▸ Other than size, what is one thing that is different about baby horses and adult horses?
  - ▸ What is one thing that is similar about baby and adult horses?

Credits:
Cover, © Byrdyak/iStock; 3, © Isselee/Dreamstime; 5, © pfluegler-photo/Shutterstock; 6-7, © helovi/iStock; 8-9, © WILDLIFE GmbH/Alamy Stock Photo; 10-11, © Andrew Twort/Alamy Stock Photo; 12-13, © Kotin/Shutterstock; 14, © Erica Hollingshead/Shutterstock; 15, © Naletova Elena/Shutterstock; 16-17, © Osetrik/Shutterstock; 18, © Nadezda Razvodovska/Dreamstime; 20-21, © Abramova_Kseniya/iStock; 22, © Maria Itina/Dreamstime; 23TL, © Rebecca Hermanson/Dreamstime; 23TR, © Miroslav Hlavko/Dreamstime; 23BL, © gadag/Shutterstock; and 23BR, © Zuzule/iStock.

Library of Congress Cataloging-in-Publication Data

Names: Shanley, Margaret, 1972- author.
Title: Baby horses / by Margaret Shanley.
Description: Bearcub books edition. | Minneapolis, Minnesota: Bearport
  Publishing Company, [2021] | Series: Animal babies | Includes
  bibliographical references and index.
Identifiers: LCCN 2020015856 (print) | LCCN 2020015857 (ebook) | ISBN
  9781642809589 (library binding) | ISBN 9781642809657 (paperback) | ISBN
  9781642809725 (ebook)
Subjects: LCSH: Foals—Juvenile literature.
Classification: LCC SF302 .S53 2021 (print) | LCC SF302 (ebook) | DDC
  636.1—dc23
LC record available at https://lccn.loc.gov/2020015856
LC ebook record available at https://lccn.loc.gov/2020015857

For more information, write to Bearport Publishing, 5357 Penn Avenue South, Minneapolis, MN 55419.

Printed in the United States of America.

Contents

It's a Baby Horse!

Plop!

Something big drops from a mother horse.

It is her baby!

It takes only a few minutes for the **foal** to be born.

Right away, the mother horse begins to lick her baby.

This cleans the foal.

After about an hour, the foal stands up.

Its legs are long and skinny.

They are almost as long as its mother's legs.

What a tall baby!

The foal takes its first steps.

It falls down a few times.

Whoops!

It tries again!

11

It is time to eat!

The baby goes to its mother.

It drinks milk from her body.

The milk will help the foal grow.

The foal follows its mother.

At first, they walk.

Then, they get faster.

Soon, the foal can **gallop**!

In about a week, the foal starts to eat grass.

Yum!

It still drinks its mother's milk, too.

After about six months, the foal no longer drinks milk.

It is growing up!

When it is a year old, the horse is called a **yearling**.

When it is about two or three years old, the horse can **mate**.

The horse will have its own baby 11 months later!

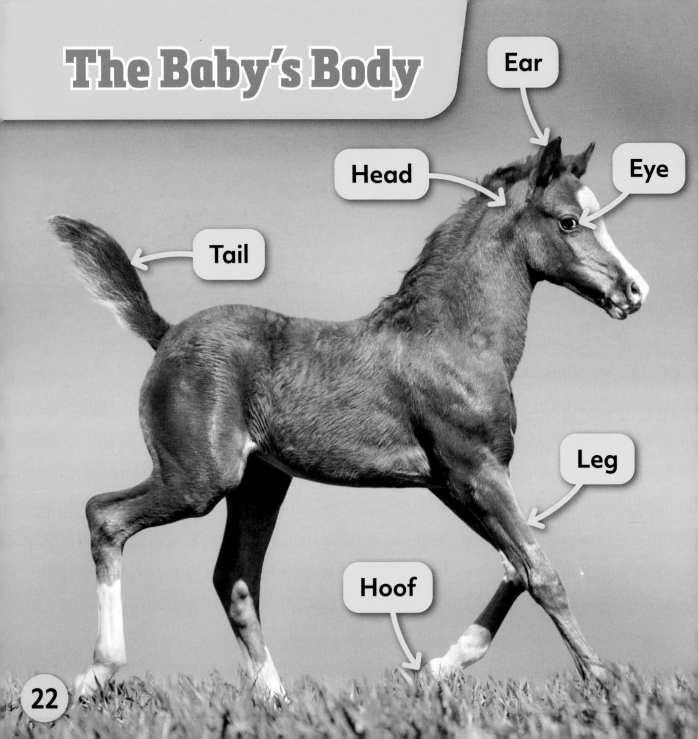

The Baby's Body

Ear

Head

Eye

Tail

Leg

Hoof

Glossary

foal a horse that is less than one year old

gallop to run fast

mate to come together to have young

yearling an animal that is one year old

Index

Read More

Gaertner, Meg. *Foals (Animal Babies).* Lake Elmo, MN: Focus Readers (2020).

Olson, Bethany. *Baby Horses (Blastoff! Readers: Super Cute!).* Minneapolis: Bellwether (2014).

Learn More Online

1. Go to **www.factsurfer.com**
2. Enter "**Baby Horses**" into the search box.
3. Click on the cover of this book to see a list of websites.

About the Author

Margaret Shanley once rode a horse named Lightning through the Arizona desert!